Poetry

to live by

MESSAGES FROM THE HEART

THE MESSENGER

Quantum Discovery
A LITERARY AGENCY

ISBN
978-1-963254-20-4 (Paperback)
978-1-963254-21-1 (eBook)

Dedicated to my mother, Miss Pearl...

What is a Mother?

What is a mother?
There aren't many things that can compare
To a mother's love and care
The qualities she possesses are O so rare.

What is a mother?
A mother is a person who is always there
She is there to listen when our souls we need to bear.

What is a mother?
A mother is a person whom we can't live without
When we have fears, she relieves our doubts.
There is a saying that when we are young, we are on their lap
When we grow older, we are on their heart
That is because a Real mother's love never parts.

So, when we think of our mother's love
Let's remember her for all the love she's shown
And the things that she has done
Because we only have one!!!!

I love you, Mama!

Table of Contents

Acknowledgements.. viii

Foreword.. ix

Life.. 2

Life's Ups and Downs 3

Families 4

Listen to Your Heart 5

Life 7

The Cycle 8

What is a Disability?.................................... 9

Love 10

Marriage 11

How Do I Love You.................................... 13

What is Marriage?....................................... 14

Friends 15

What Is Love? 16

Hey Love 17

Inspiration 18

Help the Children.......................................19

Paradise 20

New Beginnings 21

Today.. 22

Forgiving 23

Friend 24

Pray 26

Reflection **28**

    A Tribute 29

    Miss Harriete 30

    Mother 31

    My Friend 32

    Remember 33

    Sistahs 34

    Is It Because I'm Black? 35

    Wake Up 37

    Stop the Madness 38

    When Will We Really Overcome? 40

    Women 41

    I Wish 42

    Life in the New World 43

    If Things Were Different 44

    What Is A Secretary? 45

    A True Friend 46

    Families Are Forever 47

    The Beat Awards 48

    Today I Wish 49

    Our Future 50

    Why? 52

    Danny L. Smith (A Great Man) 53

    Mama and Me 55

    Now 58

Acknowledgements

I am thankful for the opportunity to publish this book. It has been
a dream of mine since 1999, when I started writing poetry.

I would like to thank my children:
TaMara and Lavonda, who both keep me grounded and serve
as listening ears when I need them. You have both grown to
be wonderful women in your own right. I also want to thank
my grandchildren, who have been the light of my life.

To my husband, Robert, who always encourages
me in whatever I endeavor to do.

There are many of you who have encouraged and pushed me to take
that leap to get this done, so I thank you...you know who you are!

Lastly, but not least, I'd like to thank my editor, Shanika,
whom without this book would not have been published.

Foreword

The pages of this book are based on my own personal experiences. They consist of Life, Love, Inspiration, and Reflection– all which have played a part in my life experiences, as well as those of my family and friends.

I hope this book will fulfill its intended purpose to be encouraging and reflective in your past and present life, as well as help you appreciate that life doesn't have to always stay the same.

Life

Life's Ups and Downs

One minute you feel your life is going in a direction that you like.
The next minute it is full of heartache and strife.
You try real hard to fight back the tears,

You were wishing that your hopes and dreams would come to past,
That you would have the happiness that you hoped for at last.
Life is full of ups and downs, hurt and pain.
Sometimes it seems as though things will never be the same.

You feel that it is over.
But you tell yourself it's not so,
Hoping that maybe in time it will again start to grow.

You keep telling yourself it's going to be ok,
But at the same time, you wish there was a better way.
Wishing for the day when the pain will be gone to stay.

Life has a way of putting us to the test,
At these times, we have to do our best
And pray that God will do the rest.

Life is full of ups and downs, hurt and pain,
But if we do the right thing
We have nothing to lose
But everything to gain

Families

Families are like dishes
They can sometimes be broken
But that doesn't take away from the value
they had when they were whole
Things happen that can cause families to fall apart
But that doesn't mean that they still aren't a family at heart

Families who are broken still need
Love and encouragement to help get them through
That's what friends should be there to do
Don't stand on the outside looking in
Be a companion, a confidant, a true friend

Marriages that end are called "failed", not "finished"
Because through thick and thin
We are supposed to be in it to win it
For our children we beat our swords in plowshares
So, we as parents, their accomplishment we can share

As families, we are all a "big pot"
For each family life holds a different lot
The outcome depends on what is thrown in
By ourselves, other family and friends
At times we may have a struggle
And on others have to depend
But it will all be worth it if you hold out until the end
So, although we may not physically be together
Let's pray we can always be friends.

❧

Listen to Your Heart

Listening to your heart is sometimes hard to do,
Because you think you know it
It can play tricks on you.

It may tell you something is right
And then tell you it is wrong
It can make the strongest of men wonder,
"What's really going on?"

It is important that we train our hearts in the right way
So, when it speaks to us
We can listen to what it has to say.

It's what's in our hearts that will lead us down the path to life
If we train it properly,
When we follow its direction, it won't bring us heartache or strife.

Life on this earth can be a happy experience and bring us great joy
But we have to make sure we don't treat it as if it were a toy.

We have to make sure we put into it the right stuff,
Using it to make decisions is a must
So, let's treat it with caution and fill it with love every day
By doing this, on the right path we will stay.

❧

Life

Life is full of ups and downs (sometimes more downs).
We find ourselves crying the tears of a clown
We wonder and ponder what it all means,
Sometimes wishing our lives could be one happy dream.
Sometimes it seems as though the hand life deals us isn't fair,
It often seems like more than we can bear
Making us throw our hands up and say why care,
Life is not always what we want it to be
But even during those times there is a remedy.
We can turn to God when we are distressed:
"God is for us a refuge and strength, a help that is readily to be found during distresses" Psalms 46:1
He never fails us; his love is the best. He can help us make it through any test.

God also made other people so that we can have friends
I hope I can be that friend for you when you seem to be at your wits end.
So, from one friend to another, trust in Jehovah
And he will help you with all of your troubles.

The Cycle

The perpetrator makes you think that you can't when you know you can.
He robs you of your life, dignity, and self-esteem
And sometimes even your family and friends.
It seems as though the vicious cycle will never end.

Domestic violence is a serious crime.
It's happening to more and more women all the time.
It robs you of who you are.
It leaves many emotional and physical scars.

Domestic violence tears families apart,
It feels as though someone has snatched out your heart.
Our children are affected,
They don't understand,
They know this person as their dad and not some crazy man.

It leaves you feeling as though your life is no good.
You just wish that others understood.
Rather than saying, "Why doesn't she leave? What is taking her so long?"
Why not ask, "What can I do to help her to move on?"

Domestic violence is not a joke.
It is not for us to ask why,
But to lend a helping hand,
A shoulder when they need to cry.

We are our brother's keeper, you see.
Maybe help to end the vicious cycle can come from you and me.
We cannot save them all,
But if we lend a helping hand,
It can help the wide gap seem small
And help to end the vicious cycle once and for all.

❦

What is a Disability?

Disability: The condition or state of being mentally or physically disabled or unable; A weakness

1. We all have a disability
    Of one sort or another
    But that doesn't mean
    We can't help ourselves or others

2. Some disabilities are large
    Others are small
    No matter what ours may be
    We still have room to grow
    So, let's not feel sorry for ourselves
    Or make excuses
    But Go, Go, Go!

3. No matter what our handicap or disability may be
    Let's strive to work hard
    To be the best we can be

4. So, the disability may not leave
    But if you work hard
    Things can get better
    Try it and see

Love

Marriage

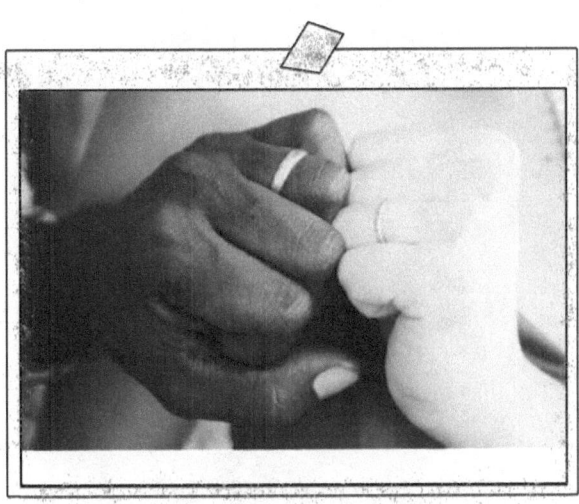

Marriage is an institution from God
Where the two of you are to become one
Working together you can accomplish a job well done.

You should take, serious, your vows,
"Until death do us part,"
Striving to love one another with all your hearts.

Marriage is a serious thing
if you don't take it lightly,
Much joy and happiness to you it will bring.

To your own mate you should cling
By doing so you can experience the saying,
"Love is a many splendid things."

So, when things get rough,
As they sometimes will,
Remember to put God in your life

And he will help you climb those hills.

So, remember that marriage is a big step
And take your vows seriously,
And God will do the rest.

How Do I Love You

How do I love you? Let me count the ways.
I love your smile, your warm embrace, your touch,
When I'm feeling down, it means so much.
You say the right things to keep my thoughts in line
When I feel myself falling, you are there to catch me every time.
I love the way you caress my body
You define every line.
Sometimes you make me feel so good, I wonder if it is a crime.
Love is a many splendid things, I've been told
After knowing you, I believe it with all my soul.
Sometimes I wonder what it would be like without you in my life
It's hard to imagine
I hope I won't ever have to find out
I know it would be tragic.
So, at times when you're feeling down and
feeling that no one seems to care,
Just remember, to show my appreciation, I will always be there.
So, together, let's keep our hearts and minds on track
Because as the saying goes,
I believe that loving you is where it's at.

What is Marriage?

Marriage is a gift from God.
Of course, there will be some ups and downs
But if you keep God in your marriage
He will help you stay rooted
And keep your marriage firmly planted on solid ground.

Husbands should love their wives
As they do themselves.
Wives should have deep respect for their husbands
And the two should put each other before anyone else

No one said that marriage would be easy.
There will always be some test.
But if you listen and have faith in one another
The challenges will be less.
If you keep the love you had for your mate at first
It will continue to grow and not get worse.

So, if you follow these tips
I have given to you
You will have many happy years of marriage
And God's blessings too.

Friends

Thanks for helping my daughter
When she needed your care.
Lending your help, making sure her cupboards were never bare.
When she felt down and out
You helped her appreciate
In Jehovah's heart she was never left out
And that he loved her without a doubt.
You showed her what true friends
And real love is all about.
Thanks for being there for my daughter
When she needed a friend.
That's the beauty of being in Jehovah's organization
You have true friends on whom you can depend
Real friendships that will never end.

❧

Thanks for being TaMara's friend

What Is Love?

Some have said that love is just a silly game that people play.
But when we fall in love, we want it to last forever, always.

We want to share with our mates our deepest emotions and thoughts
So, when we are struggling, they can help us straighten things out.

The institution of marriage can be a beautiful thing.
We want to think with our hearts and minds
So, when things are rough, we can work them out in due time.

We need to be willing to give as well as take,
If we do this, we can overlook each other's mistakes.

Love is not always 50/50
Sometimes one has to give a little more to help even the score.

So, when you get mad at each other
And you will
Just think that it's your mate's time to be stupid
And look at it as No Big Deal!

❦

The Messenger

Hey Love

Hey love, what was it about me that made you stop and stare?
Was it the way I walked, my body, my looks, my hair?
Or did I stand out like a jewel so rare?
Hey love, after seeing me, what was it that made
you want to get to know me better?
You've won my heart, so now I guess it really doesn't matter.
Hey love, let me tell you what helped you to win my heart.
You acted like a gentleman right from the start.
Although we had some problems, you always seemed to care.
I could always count on you when my soul I needed to bear.
You are like a diamond in the ruff,
I can always count on you when things get tough.
I felt that when I met you, I made the "Big Score",
So, I hope we can keep this love growing forever more.
So, hey love, let's not forget the love that we share,
Because we have a love beyond compare.

Hey Love!

❧

Inspiration

Help the Children

Somewhere along the line many of Our Children have lost their way.
They face crime, violence, hatred, and a lack of love every day.
We need to do more than shake our heads in dismay,
We need to help Our Children see that there is a better way.

Many of us may ask, "How can we help, in what way?"
There are many things that we can do to help them.
Start a productive life to have a better day.

First, we can help them to see there is more to
life than hatred, heartache, and strife.
Second, we can find time to give of ourselves,
We need to be there when there is no one else.

We need to stop pushing Our Children off on others,
Start being better mothers, fathers, sisters, and brothers.

We don't have time to waste,
We need to help children of all races find their places...
Black, red, yellow, or white,
We need to all work together to win this fight.

So, the next time a child comes to you, take a little time to listen,
Find out what you can do.
Our Children are our future, so they need a good start,
So, let's strive to help them with all our hearts.

Paradise

If everyone loved Jehovah
What a wonderful world this would be,
There would be none of the crime, jealousy, or hatred that we see
Everyone would be one big happy family.

You may say, "this can never be",
But in the near future this is exactly what we will see,
There will be no suicide at this time
Everyone will be pleased with who they are
Because we will be a perfect people by far.

This will be a time when "no resident will say I am sick."
"All the people of the land will be pardoned
for their errors" if they repent

You may say, "this sounds too good to be true."
The Bible says of Jehovah and Jesus, "this means
everlasting life, taking in knowledge of you."
If you are interested in learning about this, here's what you need to do.

Study God's word…the Bible
And apply it in your life
And before you know it, your life will have less strife.
Once you are on that road, you will see if you trust in Jehovah
You can be there eternally.

Don't take my word for it,
Look into it for yourself
And you will see on this road
You can live in paradise eternally.

❧

New Beginnings

Look around you,
What do you see?
I see people who look like you and me.
When we look at people
We should not look at race,
We should look at them as just another human with a face.

God made us all equal
Not one to be superior to the other.
He did not create us to be divided
But all as brothers.
Stop looking around to see what you can get,
But rather what you can give.
If we all do this,
The world will be a better place to live.

Stop looking at your neighbor
Thinking that you are better than he or she,
But think about what you can do to make the world a better place
For you and me.
If you take to heart these things that I have said,
The world will be a place people will want to live, not dread.

With a new attitude, you can have new hope.
As I said before, let's not look at what we can get
But what we can give
To make the world a safe, productive and happy place to live.

❦

Today

Today you're feeling down,
As though you're crying the tears of a clown.
Don't worry, you'll be alright,
If he doesn't get himself together,
Soon he'll be just another sight.

Right now, you feel that you love him,
And that there can be no other.
Don't worry if it's not him,
You'll find someone who will be a friend and a lover.

Remember to take one day at a time,
Stay busy, visit friends, do things that will ease your mind.
Most of all, have faith in yourself and keep up your self-esteem.
After a while he'll only be a memory,
Nothing more than a bad dream.

You were happy before you met him.
You'll be happy after he's gone.
I don't have to tell you,
You know that life does go on.

So, remember the person you are
And the person that you can be.
If you do this, you'll be happy again
Just you wait and see.

❧

Forgiving

He says he's leaving to make a better life,
It won't be until later that you realize he's leaving his children and wife.
Years go by and you cherish him from afar,
How happy you are on some weekends when
you look out and see his car.
When he comes home you are so happy to see him,
This soon turns into sorrow when he leaves again.

Years go by and now you are grown
And you have children of your own.
But this still doesn't stop you
From wishing he was back home.
Through the years and tears
You've forgiven him
Because no matter what
He's still your daddy dear.

You're older now and have learned
To accept things for what they are,
He's still your dad whether near or far.
In the past he did what he thought was best,
Now it's time to let sleeping dogs rest.
In the end, it doesn't matter what we think
Or feel because God above is the final judge
And he knows the real deal.

Friend

Michael was a son, brother, nephew,
Cousin, grandson and friend.
The memories we have of him
We will keep until the end.
So, let's keep our thoughts special
When we think of him.

For some of you he was someone
With whom you would fight.
As brothers and sisters do.
But you would make sure everything was right
When you were through.

For some of you he was a right-hand man.
When you were down, he would help you stand.

Michael was a good person through and through.
Although he didn't have much
He would do what he could for you.
His love and kindness always showed through.

So when you have days that are rough on you,
Think of his good qualities
And with God's help
You will make it through.
We never know what life will bring from day to day,
But when we feel weak, we can always pray.

So, now rest my dear brother,
For it won't be long
Until Jehovah God awakens you
To enjoy your new home,
Where all the things that cause hurt, pain, and sorrow will be gone.

So, for those of you who will have rough days,
And you will;
Remember God's promises
For they are real.

Pray

When things weigh heavy on your heart
And won't go away,
Fall on your knees and pray

When troublesome things are on your mind
And they want to stay,
Fall on your knees and pray

When your body is wracked with pain and disease
And you feel that no one cares,
Fall on your knees in prayer

There are a lot of things that doctors, lawyers and others can't repair,
But you can always fall on your knees
And go to your heavenly father in prayer

The Bible tells is that God is for us
A refuge and strength during distress
If you fall on your knees in prayer
God will take care of the rest

The Messenger

When the strains of this life wear you down
And get to be more than you think you can bear
God will be there for you
If you fall on your knees to him in prayer

Reflection

A Tribute

A true mom is like a rare jewel…
Nothing can compare.
When you need her help, she is always there.

A true mom puts her children's needs ahead of her own…
No matter what the situation,
She never leaves you alone.

A true mom is a rare find indeed…
She never lets you go without.
She looks after your every need.

Today we are not speaking of just any mom,
We are speaking about Mary Allen,
The "Crown Jewel".
When it comes to rearing children,
She wrote the rules.

M-motherly is the way we all knew her to be.
A-always lending a helping hand to anyone in need.
R-resilient, always strong, not letting life's challenges
get her down. She was always a joy to be around.
Y-yes, yes, she loved us all so dear; yes, we
will miss her when she is not near.

Mom, you have worked hard
Now it is time for you to rest.
When it comes to being a mom,
You have passed the test.
When it comes to being a mom,
In our book, you are the best

❧

Miss Harriete

Ah! Ma Harriete…where do we start?
Everyone who knew her, young and old
She touched their hearts.

Miss Harriete is what she was affectionately called.
There was never a stranger in her home—she welcomed one and all.
How happy she would be when friends from the'hood would call
She was a loving mother, grandmother, aunt, cousin, and friend.

If she could help you, she would be there until the end.
Ah…but don't mess with her kids because them she would defend.
Miss Harriete was a strong proud woman and mother,
When it came to handling her business, she was like no other.

To know her was to love her,
To her children, other than God, there was no one above her.
Miss Harriete was the kind of person you could sit down and
tell your troubles to, sometimes she would even cry with you.

For those of us who knew and loved her, it has left a hole in our hearts,
But the memories we have will never part.
So family, when you are feeling down and blue, look
out for one another as she taught you to do.

When your hearts get heavy and the thought of
her being gone is more than you can bear,
Remember you can always go to God in prayer,
And as Miss Harriete was, He will always be there.

❦

Mother

A mother is the best friend a person can have.
She has a way of making you happy when you are sad.

A mother's touch can mean so much.
Her touch can say, "I love you",
"How are you today?", "Are you okay?"

A mother's touch can affect you in so many wonderful ways.
It is a small gesture but it can make your day.

Although our mother is gone, the impression she
made in our lives will forever linger on.
She sacrificed her life to make things better for us.
She did it willingly and never made a fuss.
On her love and guidance, we can always trust.

Mother, it's going to be hard now that you're gone.
If we remember and cherish the things you taught us,
They will help us be courageous and strong.

So, now to my brothers and sisters, family and friends,
I say let's be strong and help one another,
She would have wanted it that way.

So, when days are hard and you are feeling blue,
Remember her love, smile, and touch,
It will help you get through.

Our mother was the best any mother could be.
Anyone who knew her I'm sure will agree.

❧

My Friend

You were my friend from the start
Your charm, wit and warm personality won my heart.
Back then I was too blind to see
Although young in years, you were good for me.

You have a way of stilling my doubts and fears.
You have a way of drying my tears.

When my world seemed as though it was going up in flames,
You helped put the fire out.

I hope it won't be long before I can enjoy your pleasing smile
Being in your company makes the day worthwhile.

I know it's hard but don't give up or take too long
Because with or without us, Jehovah's plan still goes on.
Pray and trust in Jehovah and he can make you strong.

When it seems as though others are against you,
He will make a way out.
He can bring you comfort without a doubt.

Thanks for being my friend.
I hope our friendship will never end.

Remember

I know the days ahead won't all be bright and cheerful
Many of them will be sad and tearful.
No matter how long we have our loved ones here
Life seems so short when we lose someone dear.

Although this life can be filled with bitter sorrow
For those of us who trust in God we know
that there is a better tomorrow.
We know that God will not put on us more than we can bear
This thought can always bring you comfort when you feel despair.

So, when you are feeling down, remember Darryl's love,
His smile, his loving touch,
All the things that meant so much.

So, when days get a little tough,
And you are feeling kind of sad,
Remember you still have God
The best friend and comforter you can ever have.

Sistahs

Sistahs, Sistahs, Sistahs…
Calling all Sistahs!
Sistahs, let's show the world together what we can do.

It's time to show them it's about me and you.
For so long we've been told what we can and cannot do
But to make a difference, it's up to me and you.

No longer do we have to wait on our brothers to have our backs.
Together we can take up each other's slack.
Helping and caring for one another is the key to success.
By doing this, we can all do our best.

So, let's stop fighting and pulling each other down.
Instead, let's help each other get our feet off the ground.
So, my Sistahs, let's answer the call.
If we do, none of us will have to fall.

❧

Is It Because I'm Black?

Is it because I'm Black that I have to take the
test that don't pertain to me but
the rest?
Is it because I'm Black that I have to be better than the best?
Is it because I'm Black that people stop and stare?
Or is it because I have dreads
They think I have nappy hair?
Let me tell you, none of these things define the person
who I am or make me inferior to anyone else.
Through the test of time
I've done better than many of the rest,
As a race, I've made many inventions that I haven't been given credit for.
Let me name a few to even the score…

Because of my intellect, I have contributed to saving the lives of many.
Although I was known as the Peanut Man, I had many more skills.
It wasn't money, but people of all races who were important to me.
That is why of all the things I accomplished, I only patented three.
If that isn't enough, I will give you one more to help even the score…

I save the lives of servicemen after a tunnel explosion
under Lake Erie when other rescue attempts failed.
I put my life on the line so others could be well.
So, the next time you want to put me down,
Think of where you and I would be if these inventions were not around.
And if this isn't enough to help even the score,
This is only Part I…Part II will have more.

Wake Up

Wake Up! Wake UP!
The time is here
For us to work together as brothers and sisters
Because our deliverance is near

Gone is the time for stabbing one another in the back.
It is time we as Black folks get our lives back on track.
Gone is the time for killing our brothers,
Leaving a lot of sad families and mothers.
Gone is the time for raping our sisters and putting them on the street,
Treating them as though they were just pieces of meat.
Gone is the time for selling our brothers and sisters drugs,
Leaving them to the streets to become street walkers and thugs.

Now is the time to educate our children about the ways of life
So that they won't have to deal with the toil and strife.
Again, I say, Wake Up! Wake UP!
Now is the time for we, as Black folks, to get ourselves in line.

Stop the Madness

Madness: the state of being mentally ill, especially
severely; extremely foolish behavior

Why, oh why, do so many of our young men and women have to die?
Leaving their friends and family shaking their heads in dismay
Wishing and hoping for better days!
Stop the Madness

God made us in his image
And he gave us free will
Tell me, why are we using it
To hurt one another
What is the deal?
Stop the Madness

He also created us with his attributes
Love, Justice, Wisdom and Power.
He gave us power to help lift each other up
When we may be down, not to step
One another when we are on the ground
Stop the Madness

He created us with his justice (genuine respect for others)
How can we say we are living according to this attribute when we are
taking others from their families, mothers, fathers, sisters, and brothers?
Stop the Madness

He gave us wisdom, applied knowledge, good judgement
How can we say we are using it when we are making
decisions to harm, not help our brothers?
Stop the Madness

Last but not least, he created us with his most precious attribute
which is love (a great interest in something or someone)
Treating each other the way we would treat ourselves
If we did this, we wouldn't always be hearing bad news
Things that tear us down
Instead we would be joyful
Not crying the tears of a clown
Stop the Madness

So, my brothers and sisters, family and friends
I hope you take these words seriously
Because what I am saying is true
And do what you can do to
Stop the Madness

When Will We Really Overcome?

Children are on the street,
Crying, dying every day.
Drugs, fighting, and guns
Are taking our sons and daughters away.
Lord, when will there be a better day?

Children are killing their parents
Because they try to give them discipline.
Then they end up in a place where they're
beat and raped again and again.
Lord, when will it end?
When will we really overcome?

Mothers are abusing themselves,
And their children for a rock.
Giving up everything
Their children don't even have socks.

Their children are filthy without a bath,
Left on their own—how long will they last?
When will we really overcome?

Husbands and fathers are leaving
Their children and wives,
Looking for something they feel
Will be better on the other side.
Shirking their responsibilities
Looking for an easy ride.
When will we really overcome?

Not until the day we,
As mothers, fathers, daughters and sons,
Start to love each other and live as one.
Then and only then,
Will we really overcome.

Women

Women are an asset to the human race.
We live with honor, dignity, respect and grace.
Without women,
This world would be a far different place.

From early on we as women had to struggle
To be treated as equal.
To show the world that we are a strong, valuable, and productive people.

Given a chance at success,
Many times over, we have passed the test.
We have helped our men through many a struggle,
Husbands, fathers, and even brothers.

It is time for that glass ceiling to be broken.
Time to stop giving us jobs as tokens.

It is time that we are treated
As the strong people that we are,
Because without our contributions,
This world would be a different place
By far.

I Wish

Definition (verb.): Feel or express a strong desire or
hope for something that is not easily obtainable; want
something that cannot or probably will not happen.

I wish I would have taken the chance to have a true romance
One that would fill my heart with joy and laughter, not sorrow.
Wishing things were different with each tomorrow
Not wishing that happiness would come by chance.
Wishing for a relationship that would have made my life enhanced.

I can't go back, so I just try to do the right thing from day to day
Many times, I fake it, trying my best to make it.
I wish I would have fallen in love, not just lust
Now I'm just doing things because it's a must.

Sometimes it's hard
Wishing that you could have a relationship
Built on love and trust
Not feeling at time it's just a bust

Wishing for a relationship that you really want to last
Not one you wish was in the past
I wish, I think, I dream about
How life could be if I had chosen differently
Then I have to come back to reality
And try to make my selection the best it can be
I Wish!

❧

Life in the New World

Life in this world is short it may seem.
I know it is hard but try to reflect on the day when all of this will be
As though it was just a bad dream.

Think of the time when Jehovah promises that there will be no
Sickness or death,
When we will welcome back our loved ones from their rest.

God's word tells us that death is an enemy to all.
Try to reflect on the time
When we or none of our loved ones will fall.

The Bible tells us that Jehovah is there for us
In times of distress
If you lean on his big strong arm
His holy spirit will get you through this test.

So, my friends, cry and mourn if you must,
But remember Jehovah will get you through this
If in him you put your faith and trust.

If Things Were Different

If things were different, you would be the one.
I'd enjoy your company from sunup
Until the day was done.
If you weren't around,
The thought of you would be enough to carry me through.

In the evening I would find joy in seeing your smiling face.
At night I would find comfort in your warm embrace.

But because things are not different,
These thoughts will only be a dream.
I can only feel in my heart and mind
What they could truly mean.

No matter what happens,
I hope we will always be friends.
I hope we will be there for each other,
Through thick and thin.

I hope no matter where we are
Or how far,
We will keep a special place for each other
In our hearts.

What Is A Secretary?

A secretary is a mother, nurse, doctor, a friend and confidant.
She tries to settle the problems that she not only gets from her boss
But all the teachers and little runts.

On most days she handles her affairs with care
But she can be a bit touchy if you get in her hair.

She runs the office with much skill and grace
Doing whatever she can to make it an efficient place.

It is wonderful to have a secretary as nice, friendly, and caring as you
Who has dignity and takes pride in all you do.

Thanks for being a great secretary!!

A True Friend

Carolyn was a person of integrity.
I can say that from experience because that is what she was for me.
Not only for me, but for many.
She had a big heart and she gave plenty.
If you needed something and she didn't have it
She would figure out a way to get it just so
she could help brighten your day.
She was a friend when you needed a shoulder to cry on.
When you didn't know which way to turn
If you listened to her wisdom,
There were things that you could learn.
At times she wouldn't say a word.
She would just listen.
But you always knew that you had her rapt attention.
Carolyn had a wit that was unique.
When she spoke, your interest she would peak.
She didn't let her education go to her head.
She would use it to help others instead.
Carolyn loved her family from the bottom of her heart.
We had many conversations about this
So, I can say this without a doubt
If Carolyn were here today
She would tell you what I'm saying
In her own special way.
With a big smile and sincerity of heart
Carolyn would say,
Don't worry or cry, just pray.
Think about the time when we will all be together again
And the word "goodbye" we will never have to say.

❧

Families Are Forever

Families are forever
This is true
Even at death
The thought of them never leave you.

Families are forever
This is true
Even when they make you upset
That doesn't change the fact
That they are kin to you.

Families are forever
This is true
Families were created
To help one another out
But at times you will have problems
Without a doubt.

So, at those times
Think of your family as a gift from God
And remember, this is true
You can't choose your family
God chose them for you.

❦

The Beat Awards

This was my first year attending the Beat Awards.
Thanks to Paul, Jon and others
It was a real treat.
There was music, songs, and comedy
And one of my favorites, if you can't tell, poetry.

Many of the accomplishments brought the crowd to their feet
And we can't forget our host
Rob C. Riley, who helped to bring more flavor to the Skee.

My homeboy, Will Roberson,
Distinguished Gentleman extraordinaire,
Was there
And you best believe he wasn't sporting Rocawear.

Oh, it was such a BEAUTIFUL affair.
Some of the nominees were funny,
Others were sophisticated and proud.
In my eyes, I don't think we could have witnessed a better crowd.

There was laughter and there were tears
You best believed it was worth all the cheers.
So, whether you won or were a runner up
Your participation meant much.

So, again, I say if you weren't there
You missed a real treat.
And the next time the Muskegon Beat Awards will be the place to be.

❧

Today I Wish

Today is not a good day.
Neither was yesterday.
Sometimes I think too much,
Other times I wish I could think my problems away.

The thought of things
I've done in the past
Just seem to last and last
On days like today
They make me feel real bad.
I know you can't turn back the hands of time
But it would help if I could erase these things from my mind.
I know from experience
You pay for the things you've done in the past.
I just wish the thought of it didn't have to last.

I am trying to get back to where I need to be
The thoughts of my past don't seem to cease.
I keep praying
That the thoughts will cease.
So I can live the rest of my life in peace.

Our Future

Teachers are an asset to the world
Many times, they are not given the credit that they deserve
They spend a lot of time trying to keep their students on track
Although many times parents don't have their backs.
Teachers not only teach,
They wear many hats
They play the roles of
Mother, father, doctor, counselor and nurse.
Often when a student is in trouble,
They feel the hurt
They not only teach them academically,
But they also teach lessons that will help
them get through life successfully.
Many times, they take on their students' problems
as though they were their own,
Sometimes even taking them home.
Working with teachers for many years.
I've often seen them help, quiet,
Their students' fears.
So, when you think of teaching
Don't think of it as just another job,
Because I know of some who would give their souls
to help their students reach their goals.
And teachers, on days when you think that you can't,
Remember that you can
Because our future is in your hands.
THANK YOU!!!

❧

Why?

1. Benjamin Banneker
2. Patricia Bath
3. Charles Drew
4. Thomas Elkins
5. Phillip Emeagwali (Eveevon)
6. Frederick Jones
7. Lewis Latimer
8. Alexander Miles
9. Garrett Morgan
10. Daniel Hale Williams

What do all these people have in common?
They are all Black inventors.
We as Black people have made tremendous strides
But we have not been given the accolades that we deserve.
George Carver was a world famous chemist.
If we are not given the accolades that we feel we deserve
We can have the attitude of Mr. Carver; and I quote: "Carver's great accomplishment was that of not allowing societal prejudice to define him."
With these thoughts in mind, I wrote this poem…simply titled "Why?"

TD, 2017

Why?

Why do we as Black people have to work so hard to earn our stars?
We have made many accomplishments to no avail.
But when one of us gets in trouble, it is quick
to be known that we are in jail.

Black people have made some of the greatest inventions ever known
But at times very little credit for them is shown.
Many times we have worked hard to prove
that what we can do is the best,
But in the eyes of others, many times, we still fail the test.
Many have given their lives on the battle line
Only to be recognized posthumously after dying.
Some of us have made it possible for others to make great strides.
For example, Mary, Dorothy, Katherine helped to make it possible for
man to go t the moon. So, why for some of us, this is recent news?
Why aren't these accomplishments in our history books?
Rather than being tucked away in a cranny or nook?

We have to stop leaving our education in the hands of others.
We need to do more research to learn about the many
accomplishments of our sisters and brothers.
Why are we given the shortest month of the year to celebrate?
When, if given credit for all our accomplishments,
who knows how long it would take?

There are still many great things being accomplished by our race.
So, let's not give up, but continue to work hard
to help others recognize our place.

❧

Danny L. Smith (A Great Man)

Danny L. Smith was a great man,
His love for his family and friends was beyond compare.
He was loving, funny and witty,
You would never find him acting uppity or sedity.

Danny L. Smith was a great man,
He was always willing to lend a helping hand.
As a parent you were fortunate if your child was in his care,
His knowledge and expertise he was willing to share.

Danny L. Smith was a great man,
To know him was to love him,
If you needed his help you never had to feel
You were bugging him.

So, there will be days when life is rough
But God can get us through no matter how tough.

Although he's gone, the love we have for him will linger on.

So family, as Danny was here for many of us,
We are here for you.
So, never hesitate to call if there is anything we can do.
Danny L. Smith was a great man.
We loved him and we love you too!!!

Mama and Me

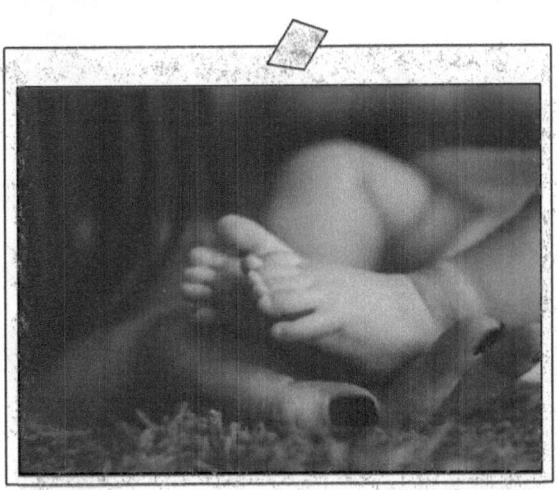

Put that iron up
You know you're not supposed to iron on Sundays
You shoulda done that yesterday;
I told you not to do that,
You don't believe fat meat greasy;
Hope without faith is like a beef steak without the gravy;
Don't slap him in his face like that,
I've never slapped you in your face;
You need to clean up that room,
Looks like a cyclone been through there;
Get up off your lazy rump and do it yourself,
Your arms and legs aren't broke;

But mama, they talking about me!
They talked about Jesus Christ,
I know you're not better than he was;
I know you ain't talkin'
If that ain't the pot calling the kettle black;
You better go somewhere and sit down and quit showing off,
Always up in grown folks' face,

Get on back outside,
They didn't come to see you;
Wipe those tears from your face or else I'm gonna
give you something to cry about;
Keep makin' that face
It's gonna get stuck like that;
No, you ain't goin',
Always wanna go somewhere,
Don't wear out your welcome,
Seldom visits make for longer friends;
You just spoiled,
Always think you're supposed to have your way;
You need to pull that skirt down,
You got it up to your rump,
Gonna catch pneumonia walking around like that;
Put something on your feet,
You're gonna get sick walking around like that;
If you get up and do something for yourself, you might feel better;
What time you get in last night?
I looked in your room
Smelled like a steel in there.

Girl, you gonna worry me to death;
Don't leave here without your jacket,
Never know when the car might break down;
I don't know who you think you're talkin' to,
I'll jump down your throat,
Upset your kidneys,
Downflow your heart,
Tap dance on your liver,
And dare your bowels to move;
Come on over here and give your mama a hug,
If I didn't mess with you, you'd think I didn't love you;
Don't quit school,
You only have one more year,
You done made it this far;

The Messenger

You can't walk around looking any kinda way,
Whatever it took to get him, it's gonna take the same thing to keep him;
Your daddy told me to put you on these;
He said you gonna go around that corner one too many times;
But mama, I ain't even thinking about that!
You know how your daddy is.

❧

Now

Now more than ever, black on black
Crime is prevalent-it's taking its tolls
Many of our brothers and sisters are losing their souls
Brothers are taking one another out without a thought
Leaving mothers and families with a lot of doubt,

Why is it that we can't all get along?
Concentrate on one another
Helping each other build happy homes.
Young men and boys think it's cool to sell drugs
and live what they feel is an easy life
Causing their mothers and families nothing but heartache and strife,

Young women and girls working the streets
Getting on drugs
Then they end up giving their bodies and souls to their John, a thug.
Life is a precious gift from God
And we should treat it as such on this Earth
If we do, life will mean so much.